Ethan Allen and the Green Mountain Boys

CORNERSTONES OF FREEDOM™

SECOND SERIES

R. Conrad Stein

Children's Press®
A Division of Scholastic Inc.
New York • Toronto • London • Auckland • Sydney
Mexico City • New Delhi • Hong Kong
Danbury, Connecticut

Photographs © 2003: Corbis Images: 9 right, 13 top, 17, 18, 33 (Bettmann), 38 (James P. Blair), 13 bottom (Darrell Gulin), 11, 44 bottom (David Muench), 21 top (Joseph Sohm/ChromoSohm Inc.), 9 left (Joseph Sohm/Visions of America); Envision/Steven Morris: 5; Fort Ticonderoga Museum: 14, 45 top left; Hulton|Archive/Getty Images: 10, 19 top, 22 top, 22 bottom, 44 top left, 44 top right; ImageState/Buddy Mays: 21 bottom; National Geographic Image Collection: 40, 41 (James P. Blair), 25 (Emory Kristof); North Wind Picture Archives: cover bottom, cover top, 3, 20, 24, 27, 31, 34, 35, 36, 39, 45 top right, 45 bottom; Photo Researchers, NY: 6 (William J. Jahoda), 19 bottom; Stock Boston/Stephen Frisch: 7 top; Superstock, Inc.: 8, 16, 32; The Image Works: 12 bottom, 12 top (Tom Brakefield), 7 bottom, 15 (color by Laura Wiley), 4 (Boyd Norton), 28 (Ted Spiegel).

Library of Congress Cataloging-in-Publication Data

Stein, R. Conrad.
  Ethan Allen and the Green Mountain Boys/R. Conrad Stein
      p. cm. — (Cornerstones of freedom. Second series)
  Summary: Discusses the facts and tall tales about Revolutionary War hero Ethan Allen, who, along with Benedict Arnold, led the Green Mountain Boys in capturing Fort Ticonderoga from the British in 1775. Includes bibliographical references and index.
      ISBN 0-516-24206-7
      1. Allen, Ethan, 1738–1789—Juvenile literature. 2. Soldiers—UnitedStates—Biography—Juvenile literature. 3. Vermont—History—To 1791—Juvenile literature. 4. Vermont—Militia—Biography—Juvenile literature. 5. Vermont—History—Revolution, 1775–1783—Campaigns—Juvenile literature. 6. United States—History—Revolution, 1775–1783—Campaigns—Juvenile literature. 7. Fort Ticonderoga (N.Y.)—Capture, 1775—Juvenile literature. [1. Allen, Ethan, 1738–1789. 2. Soldiers. 3. Vermont—History—Revolution, 1775–1783. 4. United States—History—Revolution, 1775–1783. 5. Fort Ticonderoga (N.Y.)—Capture, 1775.] I. Title. II. Series.
E207.A4 S74 2003
973.3'31'0922—dc21

                                2002009030

1 2 3 4 5 6 7 8 9 10 R 12 11 10 09 08 07 06 05 04 03

IN THE NAME OF THE GREAT
Jehovah and the Continental Congress!

— Words shouted out by the patriot Ethan
Allen as he stormed a British fort during the
American War of Independence.

ETHAN ALLEN: WHAT MANNER OF MAN?

Many tales are told about Ethan Allen. It is said that he used to pick up 100-pound (45-kilogram) sacks of flour with his teeth and swing them up on his shoulder. Once, or so the story goes, Ethan Allen fell asleep in the woods, and a rattlesnake bit him. He rose from his sleep unharmed and complained about the "cursed mosquitoes." On another occasion two enemies pounced on Allen from behind. He grabbed one in each hand and pounded them together until they begged to be let go. Fact or fiction? In the case of Ethan Allen, it can be hard to tell the difference. In Allen's life, it sometimes seems there are as many tall tales as there are solid facts.

A timber rattlesnake, typical of the type in the American woodlands

Sacks of flour similar to the one-hundred-pound sacks Ethan Allen allegedly picked up with his teeth

Certainly Ethan Allen was a key figure in the early stages of the American War of Independence. Leading a group of backwoodsmen called the Green Mountain Boys, he attacked and overpowered the British fort at Ticonderoga, New York, in May 1775. But by assaulting the fort was Allen acting as a true American patriot? Or was he just looking for a good fight?

Woodlands near Litchfield, Connecticut, as they look today

A WILDERNESS YOUTH

Ethan Allen was born on January 21, 1738, in Litchfield, Connecticut. The land of his youth was a raw country of forests and wild game, well suited to the Allen clan's way of life. The first of the Allen family emigrated from England to the New World in 1632. True pioneers, the Allens always sought fresh land upon which to build their dreams.

Young Ethan was not only the biggest boy in his log cabin community but also the brightest. He learned to read at an early age by mastering the only book that most colonial families had in their homes—the Bible. Ethan did so well in reading and writing that his family made plans to send him to Yale College. Those plans were dashed when his father died suddenly in 1755. Ethan was the eldest of eight brothers and

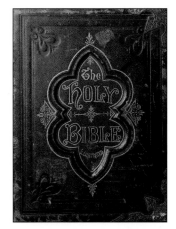

Practically every colonial American household owned an old Bible like this one.

The original thirteen colonies

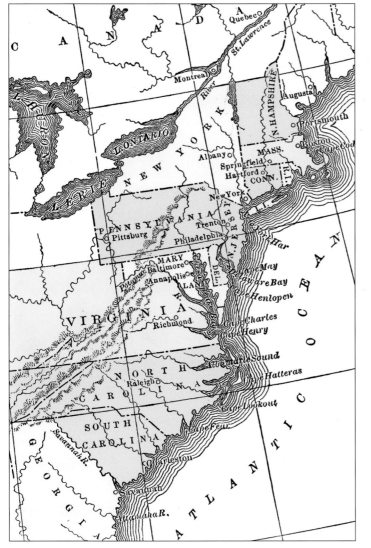

THE THIRTEEN ENGLISH COLONIES

At the time of Ethan Allen's birth the thirteen colonies were well established along North America's eastern seaboard. The original thirteen colonies were (from north to south): New Hampshire, Massachusetts, Rhode Island, Connecticut, New York, New Jersey, Pennsylvania, Delaware, Maryland, Virginia, North Carolina, South Carolina, and Georgia. Settlement of the region began in the 1600s, and by 1750 the population of the thirteen colonies totalled about one million settlers, most of whom came originally from England.

HISTORIC YALE

Yale College (now Yale University) was established in 1701. Situated in New Haven, Connecticut, Yale is the third-oldest institution of higher learning in the United States. Only Harvard (founded in 1636) and the College of William and Mary (1693) are older.

sisters, and he had to support the family. He was largely self-taught. As he once wrote, "[I] had to acquire the knowledge of grammar and language, as well as the art of reasoning, principally from a studious application to it . . ."

As a young man, Allen studied a religious philosophy called **Deism,** which was popular among intellectuals in the colonies. Deists held that God created the universe in much the same manner as a master clockmaker makes a perfect clock. Once completed, God—like the clockmaker—exercises little influence over His final creation. Therefore, Deists believed that humans should seek God not through prayer, but by observing the natural wonders found on earth. While many educated people in the colonies found truth in Deism, the average farmer or worker rejected the philosophy. Deism seemed to lessen God's role in the order of the universe. Allen's decision to become a Deist produced sharp arguments between him and his working-class friends and neighbors.

Thomas Jefferson, the principal author of the Declaration of Independence, also studied Deism. The philosophy of Deism can be seen in Jefferson's statement that the colonies declared independence by authority of ". . . the Laws of Nature and of Nature's God . . ."

Thomas Jefferson and his creation, the Declaration of Independence

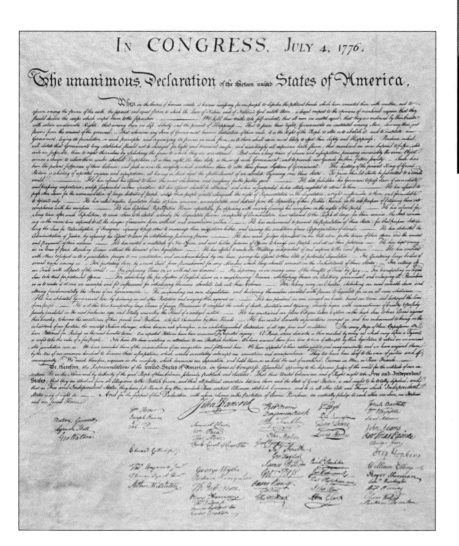

Statue of Ethan Allen representing Vermont in the Capitol at Washington, D.C.

At age twenty-four, Allen married a girl named Mary Bronson. The couple had several children. Quite likely, Allen neglected his family, as he was constantly on the go, scouting out new territory and launching business ventures. Around 1770 the Allens moved to a wild region called the New Hampshire Grants. Rumors hinted that Allen left Connecticut because he got into a fight with another man and was wanted by the law. In one way, however, the story seems unlikely: Who in the world would want to fight Ethan Allen? He was a giant, standing 6 feet, 5 inches (1.96 meters) at a time when a man of 5 feet, 10 inches (1.78 m) was considered tall. Neighbors claimed Allen was as strong as a workhorse.

AT WAR WITH THE YORKERS

The area called the New Hampshire Grants is now the state of Vermont. In the 1770s the "Grants" was a disputed territory, claimed by the colonies of New Hampshire and New York. The Grants' most distinguished feature was the beautiful Green Mountain range, which ran down its middle like a spine. This was the sort of land Allen responded to—rugged, untamed, and posing a challenge to a settler. For the rest of his life he would love the Green Mountain country.

The lovely Green Mountain country in today's state of Vermont

WHAT'S IN A NAME?

The Green Mountains were so named by early French explorers who were impressed by the lush forests they found there. The name "Vermont" is derived from the French words *vert* (green) and *mont* (mountain). Ethan Allen's close

The whitetail deer (above) and the ruffled grouse (below) are among the many animals that live in Vermont's Green Mountains.

friend, Dr. Thomas Young, was the first person to suggest calling the region Vermont. Modern Vermont is nicknamed "The Green Mountain State."

Portions of the Green Mountains remain as unspoiled today as when Ethan Allen first saw them. Spread over 360,000 acres (1,457 square kilometers) in Vermont is the lovely Green Mountain National Forest. In this exciting woodland live white-tailed deer, black bear, ruffed grouse, and other game animals. Miles of hiking trails challenge visitors.

One of the liveliest places in the Grants was the Catamount Tavern in the village of Bennington. **Catamount** is the folk name given to the mountain lions that roamed the American wilderness. Another story told about Ethan Allen involves an encounter with one of these wildcats. It was said that one night while Allen was walking home from the tavern, a catamount leaped from a tree and landed on

Dr. Thomas Young, Ethan Allen's friend and teacher

Mountain lions, called catamounts in the old days, once roamed the American wilderness in great numbers.

his back. Enraged, he strangled the animal with his bare hands. Truth or **folklore?** Who knows. It is known that outside the Bennington tavern was a stuffed catamount perched on a tall pole. Interestingly, the snarling mountain lion faced west—toward New York.

By 1770 hundreds of settlers had established farms in the New Hampshire Grants. Colonial leaders from New York claimed this land belonged to them and said the settlers there were **squatters**, or illegal residents. Many lawyers in the colonies agreed with New York's claims. Boundaries between the colonies were loosely drawn in those days, and land disputes were common. Still, the Grants farmers—legally or illegally—were determined to stay on the land they considered theirs. To protect themselves from powerful "Yorkers," the farmers organized a loose-knit army they called the Green Mountain Boys. Their commander was Ethan Allen, whom the Boys had given the rank of colonel.

Who were the Green Mountain Boys? They were not a true army. None of them owned anything resembling a uniform. But they were well armed. Most carried the Pennsylvania

Ethan Allen's own rifle

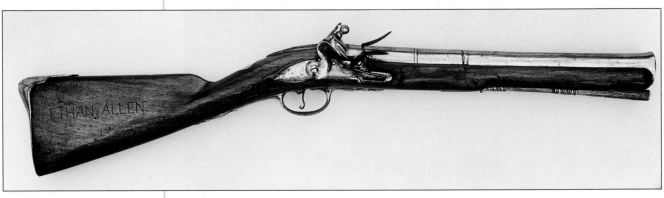

rifle, a deadly accurate weapon that measured almost 6 feet (1.83 m) in length. Hunting was not a sport to these pioneers. They all hunted to feed their families. Many claimed they could hit a squirrel in the eye at fifty paces.

The war with the Yorkers was largely a war of words, as both sides were locked in endless arguments. Ethan Allen was the principal spokesman for the Grants farmers during conferences with the Yorkers. Allen was a skilled debater, who drew upon his studies of religion and philosophy to advance the farmers' cause. During one meeting the New York Attorney General tired of Allen's arguments and told him to give in because "Might often prevails against right." Always the philosopher, Allen responded by saying, "The gods of the valleys are not the same as the gods of the hills." When the Attorney General asked what this meant, Allen thundered out, "Come up to Bennington, and we'll show you."

BRIDGING HISTORY

Vermonters are proud of the 114 covered wooden bridges that span their state's rivers and streams. The bridges have slanting roofs to prevent snow buildup, which could cause the structure to sag. Many of these bridges have deep roots in state history. The Henry Bridge at Bennington is the site where the Green Mountain Boys confronted the New York posse in 1771. The original bridge stood for more than two hundred years before it was completely rebuilt in 1989.

Finally the Yorkers grew tired of debating. In 1771 a New York sheriff named Henry Ten Eyck came to Bennington with a **posse** of three hundred men. The sheriff was determined to teach the rebels in the Grants a lesson they would never forget. The Green Mountain Boys met the posse at the foot of a covered bridge. Few words were exchanged. Instead, the Boys stood silently clutching their rifles and greeting the Yorkers with hard stares. Acting brave, the sheriff marched resolutely into this menacing group. He failed to notice that to his rear the frightened posse members had drifted away in twos and threes. The sheriff finally turned and realized he was virtually alone. At that point the sheriff retreated across the bridge.

Allen and the Boys delighted in humiliating their foes. Once they tied a pro-New York settler to a chair, hauled him to the top of the 20-foot (6.1-m) pole in front of the Catamount Tavern, and kept him there, kicking and screaming, for two hours. On another occasion the Boys caught two Yorker sheriffs and imprisoned them in separate rooms on the same side of a house. That night they ordered the prisoners to look out their windows. The sheriffs saw a figure hung by the neck dangling from a tree limb. The Boys told each sheriff that the hanged victim was his companion. Actually, the object swinging from the limb was a straw man, craftily made by one of the Green Mountain Boys. The terrified sheriffs were released separately in the morning, with warnings to stay away from the Grants. The two men, each thinking the other dead, were astonished when they met on an Albany street a few days later.

The Battle at Concord, pictured here, was fought on April 19, 1775, and helped trigger the Revolutionary War.

CAUSES OF THE WAR

For more than 150 years the American colonists lived in harmony with their mother country, England. Problems developed after the French and Indian War, which ended in 1763. The war drained the English treasury. To raise money, the government began to tax the American colonies. The colonists objected to taxation because they had no representatives in the English **Parliament** (the legislative body in England). Without representatives in Parliament, there was no one in the English government to argue the colonial cause and perhaps reduce the tax burden of the colonists. Throughout the American colonies angry men and women shouted out the now famous charge, "Taxation without representation is tyranny!" This bitter dispute over taxes and representation contributed to the outbreak of the American Revolutionary War.

★ ★ ★ ★

The dispute with the Yorkers was soon overshadowed by a far larger and more important conflict. On April 19, 1775, shots were exchanged between colonists and British troops at the towns of Lexington and Concord in Massachusetts. The American War of Independence had begun.

"A PASSION FOR LIBERTY"

"Ever since I arrived to a state of manhood, I have felt a sincere passion for liberty," wrote Ethan Allen. From the onset of the war he and the Green Mountain Boys were soldiers in the cause of American independence. Allen called the opening battle with British troops a ". . . bloody attempt at Lexington to enslave America . . ."

In theory the colonists were led by the First Continental Congress, which met in

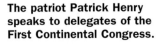
The patriot Patrick Henry speaks to delegates of the First Continental Congress.

A battle scene from the French and Indian War. Wars around the globe drained England's treasury and caused it to tax the American colonies for the first time.

Philadelphia in 1774. In practice, however, local authorities took charge. A lack of central authority led to mix-ups in commands, as would soon be seen in Ethan Allen's first military adventure. Days after the battles at Lexington and Concord, a Connecticut group called the Revolutionary Committee of Correspondence asked Ethan Allen to march north from Bennington and attack the British at Fort Ticonderoga. In a note, the Committee added that the fort must be assaulted at once.

Allen chose his best runner, a blacksmith named Gershom Beach, to race out in the countryside and gather the Green Mountain Boys. The Boys were told to prepare for a "wolf hunt." The frontier soldiers assembled. Then a stranger entered their camp. He was Benedict Arnold, an **enigmatic** figure in American history.

Born in Connecticut, Benedict Arnold was a prosperous businessman. Because of his intelligence and his education, he was made a high-ranking officer in the Continental Army early in the war against the British. Certainly Arnold was very different in appearance from Allen. Arnold wore a fancy uniform, in contrast to Allen's frontier clothes. Yet in many

Benedict Arnold, who is widely considered to be a traitor in American history

19

A scene from Paul Revere's famous ride

respects, the two men were similar. Both were stubborn to the point of being **arrogant.** Both were courageous to the point of being foolhardy. Both men insisted on being the boss.

Unknown to Ethan Allen, Benedict Arnold had also been given orders to attack Fort Ticonderoga. Arnold's orders came from a Massachusetts group called the Committee of Safety. No doubt Arnold and Allen argued over who should be the boss. But somehow the two men—both of whom had enormous **egos**—agreed to a joint command. The small army was made up of about 150 colonists, most of whom were Green Mountain Boys.

ATTACK IN THE NIGHT

Fort Ticonderoga stood on the west bank of the southern end of Lake Champlain in northern New York. A star-shaped structure with thick stone walls, it was once the strongest fort in

VISITING HISTORY

Fort Ticonderoga was first built in 1755. After the revolution, it was a ruin for many years. In 1909 it was completely rebuilt and opened as a tourist attraction. Today the fort is a highlight of any visit to upstate New York.

North America. In British hands the fort could serve as a base from which the soldiers, known to the colonists as Redcoats, could march south toward Albany and split New York in two.

As they marched, Allen and Arnold pondered a critical question: Just how many British soldiers defended the fort? To determine this, Ethan Allen sent a spy with long, unkempt hair ahead of his army. The spy approached

Lake Champlain, in upstate New York, is sometimes called the "sixth Great Lake."

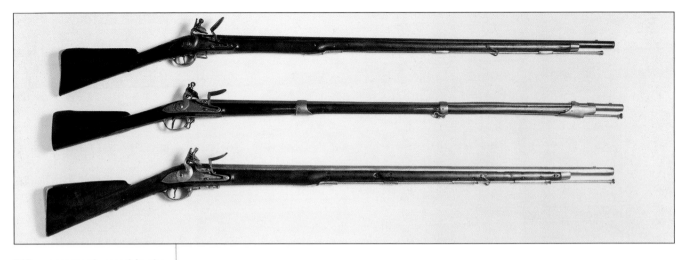

Rifles commonly used in the Revolutionary War era

British Grenadier

Ticonderoga and asked the guards if he could use the services of the army barber. The guards agreed and allowed the man inside. While getting his hair cut, the man noted that only about fifty British soldiers manned the fort. After paying the barber, the spy returned and reported this vital information to Ethan Allen.

On the banks of Lake Champlain, Allen and his raiders found two small boats. This meant only half of the already small army could participate in the assault. Before sunrise on May 10, 1775, about eighty men squeezed into the boats and rowed to the opposite shore. Once on land, Ethan Allen asked his men to raise their weapons if they were willing to risk their lives. Every man held his rifle above his head. Then, as silently as possible, the group marched toward Fort Ticonderoga.

Luck smiled on the colonists that night. Only at the last moment did a sentry notice the approaching band. The guard pointed his rifle at the obvious leader. The huge figure of

Ethan Allen made a perfect target. He pulled the trigger. The gun flashed and banged but failed to discharge its bullet. Such a "flash in the pan" misfire was common with **flintlock** firearms. In this case, the flash in the pan saved Ethan Allen's life.

The fort, now alerted, erupted with shouts and gunshots. Most of the defenders were shocked by the suddenness of the attack and surrendered without a fight. Miraculously, no one on either side was killed. Threatening a soldier with his sword, Ethan Allen ordered him to point out the commander's quarters. The frightened soldier motioned to a door. According to a British witness, Ethan Allen bellowed, "Come out of there, you . . . old rat!" A sleepy British officer opened the door with his trousers in one hand. The officer asked why and in whose name did these men barge into his fort. It was then that Ethan Allen uttered his history-making words, "In the name of the Great Jehovah and the Continental Congress."

Immediately after taking Ticonderoga, Ethan Allen and the Green

IN HIS OWN WORDS

Here is Ethan Allen's own written account of how he and his men conquered Fort Ticonderoga. Allen used words that will not be familiar to modern readers. For example, when the sentry's gun misfired, Allen wrote, "[the guard] *snapped his fusee* at me." In the report below, words in brackets have been inserted into Allen's original report to provide clarity. The writing has also been edited because Allen, and most writers of his time, believed in using long, drawn-out sentences:

> I found a sentry posted [at the gate of the fort], who instantly [fired at me but his gun did not discharge]; I ran immediately toward him, and he retreated . . . My party followed me into the fort . . . The garrison being asleep . . . we gave three huzzas [cheers] which greatly surprised them. One of the sentries made a pass at one of my officers with a charged bayonet, and slightly wounded him. My first thought was to kill [the Englishman] with my sword; but, in an instant . . . he dropped his gun and asked for quarter [offered to give up] which I readily granted him and demanded of him the place where the commanding officer [lived] . . . I ordered the commander to deliver to me the fort instantly [and] he answered by what authority I demanded it; I answered, "In the name of the great Jehovah and the Continental Congress."

American forces commanded by Colonel Henry Knox (right) hauled Fort Ticonderoga's cannons more than 300 miles to deliver them to George Washington in Boston.

Mountain Boys overwhelmed a nearby British stronghold called Crown Point. The colonists also seized Ticonderoga's cannon and gunpowder, which were later used by General George Washington to defend the city of Boston from British attack.

Hauling the big guns from Fort Ticonderoga to Boston was an epic (history-making) story in itself. The job was given to the Boston bookseller Henry Knox. Fort Knox, an army base in Kentucky, is named after him. Knox and a crew of rugged men tied the cannons onto ox-drawn sleighs and carted them 300 miles (483 km) over snowcapped mountains in what he called, "a noble train of artillery."

Crown Point, a fort near Ticonderoga, was also taken by Allen and his men.

★ ★ ★ ★

THE AFTERMATH OF VICTORY

Ethan Allen and Benedict Arnold parted company after their success at Fort Ticonderoga. Allen traveled to Philadelphia, while Arnold fought a desperate battle in the snows of Canada. Later Benedict Arnold became a notorious traitor.

In the opening stage of the Revolutionary War, Benedict Arnold was one of George Washington's most trusted commanders. However, Arnold was an ambitious man who enjoyed living far beyond his means. After five years of war Arnold had not received the promotions he thought he deserved, and he was seriously in debt to several banks. In 1780, Arnold was given command of the American fortress at West Point. Writing secret letters, Arnold offered to surrender West Point to the British for the sum of 20,000 English pounds, a small fortune in those days. This act of treachery was discovered. Benedict Arnold switched sides, served with the British Army, and finally fled to England. Today his name is scorned in American history.

Ethan Allen was bitterly disappointed because he believed he never received proper credit for his triumph at Ticonderoga. Shortly after the battle, Allen passed through Bennington. By this time all the colonies buzzed with news of his victory. Not normally a churchgoer, Allen decided to attend services in Bennington. He had heard

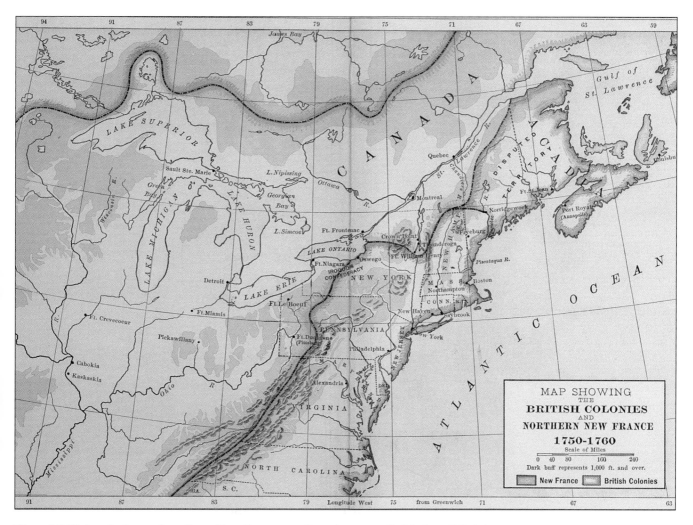

Map of British colonies and northern New France, as Canada was called before Britain's victory in the French and Indian War.

that the reverend planned to thank God for granting the colonial side such good fortune. The parson did just that—he heaped praise on God Almighty for causing the fort's downfall. Finally, according to an often-told story, Ethan Allen stood up in church and shouted out, "Aren't you going to mention the fact that I was there?"

The American military academy at West Point, which lies on the Hudson River in upstate New York

THE LEGACY OF ETHAN ALLEN

Clearly the capture of Fort Ticonderoga was the highlight of Ethan Allen's life. After that event he faced misfortune and defeat.

Allen hoped to be named commander of a regiment mostly made up of the Green Mountain Boys. But many colonial leaders looked upon him as a rebel who could not be trusted. Allen was given a small unit of scouts and sent to Canada to recruit Frenchmen for the cause of American independence. He quickly overstepped his authority. During the autumn of 1775, Allen tried to assault the city of Montreal with an army of about one hundred men. The attack failed miserably, and Ethan Allen—the hero of Ticonderoga—was taken prisoner by the British.

The British treated Allen cruelly during his captivity. He and fellow prisoners were sent to England in the hold of a rat-infested prison ship. The prisoners were given little food or water and were often chained by the ankle in painful iron braces. English soldiers guarding the prisoners delighted in threatening the captured American rebels with severe punishment. One English officer told Allen that the American revolution would soon be crushed and that all of its leaders—especially Allen—would hang. Allen later wrote, "I gave him [an] answer, that if they stayed till they conquered America, before they hanged me, *I should die of old age.*"

In all, Allen spent two and a half years as a British prisoner. It was not until May of 1778 that Allen was released as part of a prisoner exchange between the colonists and the British government. Upon Allen's return, George Washington said of Allen, "There is an original something in him that commands admiration; and his long captivity and sufferings have only served to increase, if possible, his enthusiastic zeal."

Allen wrote a book about his years as a prisoner. Reading like an adventure story, his *Captivity and Treatment by the British* was a best-seller in the colonies. Eight issues of Allen's book were printed in just two years. His accounts of British mistreatment of American prisoners fanned the flames of hatred against the mother country. He wrote about Americans being deliberately starved: "I have [seen] the prisoners in the agonies of death . . . pleading for God's sake for something to eat . . ." Allen became the leader of the captives and urged the others to be strong in the face of brutal treatment. The book became the talk of the colonies. Certainly the popular book enhanced Allen's image as a genuine hero of the American Revolution.

Allen soon wrote another book, one that caused many Americans to curse his name. As a teenager, Allen had met a doctor, named Thomas Young, who had recently graduated from Yale. Allen was impressed with Dr. Young's knowledge of religion. Young was a Deist, and Allen soon adopted Deist beliefs also. Young and Allen wrote a book explaining the principles of Deism to fellow Americans. Few people read Allen's

WHAT'S IN A TITLE?

In revolutionary times readers were unafraid of long-winded book titles. The complete title of the religious book by Ethan Allen and Dr. Thomas Young was *Reason: The Only Oracle of Man; Or, a Compenduous System of Natural religion, to which is Added Critical remarks on the Truth and Harmony of the Four Gospels with Observation on the instructions Given by Jesus Christ and on the Doctrines of Christianity.*

Ethan Allen became a hero to the colonists after his exploits during the American revolution.

book on Deism these days, but its publication infuriated churchgoing men and women in the late 1700s. According to many Americans of the time, even thinking about Deism was a sinful activity. Because of the book, a prominent preacher denounced Allen as ". . . one of [the] wickedest men [who] ever walked this guilty globe."

THE GREEN MOUNTAIN BOYS FIGHT THE BRITISH

While Allen was being held prisoner his old organization, the Green Mountain Boys, continued to wage war against the forces of Great Britain. Their finest hour came in the

As in Allen's day, the town of Bennington lies in heavily wooded country between the Taconic Mountains and the Green Mountains

summer of 1777 when the British chose to attack the town of Bennington in the heart of the Green Mountain country. Farmers in Bennington owned large herds of horses. The British commander, General John Burgoyne, hoped to commandeer, or take by force, those horses and use them to make an advance on Albany, New York. No one was going to get away with stealing horses in Bennington—not with the Green Mountain Boys around.

General Burgoyne commanded a regiment of mixed troops. Most of his men were German professional soldiers, **mercenaries,** who were paid to fight for the British. However the officers received the bulk of the pay while the common German soldiers, known as Hessians, got only a few coins for risking their lives on foreign soil. Also included in Burgoyne's forces were Native Americans from tribes that were loosely aligned with the British. This was not by anyone's definition a unified army. The field commander of the mercenary units was a German officer named Baum who spoke hardly a word of English.

British commander during the Battle of Bennington, General John Burgoyne

Hessian soldiers, marching on the left, fought against the colonists during the Revolutionary War.

Defending Bennington was a force composed of 1,500 New Hampshire men and 400 Green Mountain Boys. By contrast these American troops were a unified army, one that was determined to throw the foreigners out of their farms and villages. The Green Mountain Boys also knew the countryside surrounding Bennington. The Boys were prepared to use every glen and hill to surprise the enemy troops.

Grave problems developed for the Hessians even as they approached Bennington. Baum insisted his men march down the country road in European-style close formations. Meanwhile, Indian warriors ranged far ahead of the main column and delighted in stealing cowbells from cows grazing in pastures. Clanging cowbells alerted the American defenders of Bennington that the enemy was on the march. The New Hampshire men and the Green Mountain Boys hid in the woods alongside the road and waited for the Hessians to come in range of their rifles. American sharpshooters then picked off the mercenary soldiers as if they were target shooting. German troops, whose hearts were never in this fight, slipped into the woods to save their lives.

The Battle of Bennington was fought on August 16, 1777. It was a disaster for the British side. More than 200 soldiers, most of them German mercenaries, were killed and 700

Colonial troops march to fight in the Battle of Bennington.

were captured. The Americans suffered about eighty men killed or wounded. The battle proved that the Green Mountain Boys—even without their leader Ethan Allen—would fight like lions when defending their home grounds.

ALLEN FIGHTS THE YORKERS

Ethan Allen returned to the Green Mountain country in May 1778. He had not seen the land he loved in more than two years. In Bennington his comrades gathered to throw the one-time prisoner of the British a party. Cannon were pulled to the village green and fired a salute to honor the returning hero. Allen was ushered into the Catamount Tavern, where he heard tales of the triumphant Battle of Bennington, which had been fought eight months earlier. The party given Allen was joyous. But the country was in grave trouble.

In the spring of 1778, when Allen returned to Bennington, the Revolutionary War was three years old. Despite the victory at Bennington the conflict was not going well for George Washington and the Americans.

General George Washington was the supreme commander of the colonial forces.

36

Canada remained firmly in British hands. Fort Ticonderoga—Allen's greatest prize—had been recaptured by the British.

Even Allen's commitment to American independence came into question. At the very least, it seemed to become less important to him than independence for Vermont. The hated Yorkers still opposed Vermont's becoming a state. Allen had a group of powerful Yorkers jailed, tried, and heavily fined by a supportive judge.

Allen's most **dubious** actions came when he secretly negotiated with the British in the last years of the war. More than 10,000 British soldiers were stationed in Canada, posing an immediate threat to Vermont, which was unprotected by the Continental Army. Allen offered to make peace with the British if they recognized Vermont's independence, which it declared in 1777. Was this the act of a traitor? Was Ethan Allen another Benedict Arnold? Historians have debated this question for more than 200 years.

Some historians claim Allen made his proposal to the British in order to frighten the Continental Congress into making Vermont a state. Other historians believe Allen negotiated with the British as a means of buying time and therefore staving off an attack on Vermont. Such reasoning holds that as long as the British were talking to Allen their troops would not march on Vermont. If indeed Allen hoped to gain time by negotiating with the British, his tactic worked. The Revolutionary War ended in 1783 without the British ever occupying Vermont.

The city of Burlington, Vermont, as it looks today

END OF THE DREAM

Allen's first wife died in 1783. He then married a beautiful young woman named Francis Montresor who shared his love for reading and had his talent for wit. At the time of his second marriage, Allen still dreamed of statehood for Vermont. He told his new wife that by marrying him, she would be "queen of a new state." The Allens moved to a farm near Burlington, Vermont, where two sons and a daughter were born to them.

Once settled on his farm, Allen continued his work to achieve statehood for Vermont. In this effort he clashed with his old enemies—the politicians of New York. The Yorkers viewed Vermont as an extension of their own state. In order to attack the prospect of

THE HOMESTEAD

Near Burlington is the Ethan Allen Homestead, where Allen's 1787 farmhouse is preserved. Every year hundreds of Vermont schoolchildren visit this historic site. There they learn about the man who some call the "Robin Hood of Vermont" because of his fight for the rights of small farmers.

The Ethan Allen farmhouse at the Ethan Allen Homestead

STATEHOOD

On March 4, 1791, Vermont entered the Union as the fourteenth state. It was the first state added to the Union by the new Congress after the British colonies became a nation. In 1777, fourteen years before it was granted statehood, Vermont adopted a constitution that forbade slavery. Thus, Vermont was the first American state to outlaw the practice of slavery within its borders.

Vermont's statehood, the Yorkers attacked Ethan Allen's honesty. By this time Allen was one of Vermont's largest landowners. His enemies argued that he was working as much to protect his property as to secure statehood.

In the end, Allen would not live to see his dream of Vermont statehood fulfilled. The winter of 1789 was the hardest in memory in the Vermont woodlands. Despite roaring winds and deep snow, Allen hitched horses to a wagon and drove across frozen Lake Champlain to get a load of hay for his farm animals. During the trip he caught a fever and died. He was fifty-one years old.

News of Allen's death swept through the colonies. In the Catamount Tavern in Bennington, strong men were seen weeping. In life Allen was a giant. In death he became a legend. Allen often battled leaders of his own government, but he also fought the British and helped to secure independence for the United States.

Today, as it did in Ethan Allen's time, Lake Champlain still sometimes freezes solid in the winter.

Glossary

arrogant—an exaggerated feeling of self-importance

catamount—a name rural people once gave to wildcats such as the mountain lion or lynx

commandeer—to take goods or capture people by military force

Deism—a religious belief that acknowledges the existence of God, but that holds God does not intervene in the ordinary lives of humans

dubious—arousing doubt or uncertainty

ego—feelings of self-importance

enigmatic—a curious or mysterious person or event

flintlock—a firearm using a device in which flint in the hammer ignites gunpowder in a pan; the resulting explosion propels the bullet

folklore—stories that are passed from one generation to another which may or may not be based on a true event

Jehovah—a name given to God by many translators of the Old Testament

mercenary—a paid professional soldier who works for a foreign government

Parliament—the main governing body (similar to the U.S. Congress) in Great Britain and many other countries

posse—a group of law-enforcement officers usually led by a sheriff

squatter—a person who is illegally occupying land

Timeline: Ethan Allen and

1738	1750	1755	1763	1770	1775

1738 — Ethan Allen is born on January 21 in Litchfield, Connecticut.

1750 — The population of the thirteen colonies reaches an estimated one million settlers, most of them English.

1755 — Ethan Allen's father dies, leaving Ethan as the head of a family of eight younger brothers and sisters.

1763 — The French and Indian War ends. England is the victor; but the war has drained the English treasury, and the mother country takes measures to tax its American colonies.

1770 — Farmers form a militia they call the Green Mountain Boys. They name Allen their commander.

APRIL 19 Colonists and British troops exchange gunfire at the towns of Lexington and Concord in Massachusetts.

MAY 10 Ethan Allen and the Green Mountain Boys conquer Fort Ticonderoga.

SEPTEMBER 25 During an assault on the city of Montreal, Ethan Allen is taken prisoner by the British.

the Green Mountain Boys

1778

On May 6, as part of a prisoner exchange, Ethan Allen is released from British captivity.

1783

On September 3, the Americans and the British sign the Treaty of Paris, which officially ends the War of Independence and allows the United States to emerge as a new nation.

1789

Ethan Allen dies on February 12.

1791

Vermont becomes the fourteenth American state on March 4.

To Find Out More

BOOKS

Aronson, Virginia. *Ethan Allen: Revolutionary Hero.* Philadelphia: Chelsea House, 2001.

Gauch, Patricia. *Aaron and the Green Mountain Boys.* New York: Betterway Books, 1988.

Heinrichs, Ann. *America the Beautiful: Vermont.* Danbury, CT: Children's Press, 2001.

Kent, Deborah. *Lexington and Concord.* Danbury, CT: Children's Press, 1997.

Marrin, Albert. *The War For Independence: The Story of the American Revolution.* New York: Macmillan, 1988.

Peck, Robert Newton. *Hang For Treason.* Garden City, NJ: Doubleday, 1976.

ONLINE SITES

Ethan Allen Homestead
http://www.uvm.edu/~vhnet/hertour/ethan1.html

Ethan Allen(1738–1789)
http//www.virtualvermont.com/history/eallen.html

Vermont's Covered Bridges
http:/www.virtualvermont.com/coveredbridge

Index

About the Author

R. Conrad Stein was born and raised in Chicago. He enlisted in the United States Marines at age eighteen and served three years. He later graduated from the University of Illinois with a degree in history. Mr. Stein is a full-time author who has published more than one hundred books for young readers. He lives in Chicago with his wife (children's book author Deborah Kent) and their daughter, Janna. Traveling is Mr Stein's favorite hobby. He especially likes to follow hiking trails in wilderness areas. Several times he has hiked in Vermont's Green Mountain region, and he considers it one of the prettiest areas he has ever seen.